D0753561

Do Vampires Exist?

Other titles in the *Do They Exist?* series include:

Do They Exist?

Do Vampires Exist?

Patricia D. Netzley

ReferencePoint Press®

San Diego, CA

© 2016 ReferencePoint Press, Inc.
Printed in the United States

For more information, contact:
ReferencePoint Press, Inc.
PO Box 27779
San Diego, CA 92198
www.ReferencePointPress.com

LIBRARY OF CONGRESS CATALOGING-IN-PUBLICATION DATA

Netzley, Patricia D., author.
  Do vampires exist? / by Patricia D. Netzley.
     pages cm. -- (Do they exist?)
  Includes bibliographical references and index.
  Audience: Grade 9 to 12.
  ISBN-13: 978-1-60152-860-5 (hardback)
  ISBN-10: 1-60152-860-4 (hardback)
  1. Vampires--Juvenile literature. I. Title.
  BF1556.N48 2016
  398'.45--dc23
                                                    2015010390

Contents

A Distorted Nature

In nature some animals survive by sucking out the blood of other animals. For example, three bat species feed solely on blood. But for centuries people have feared the existence of beings who subsist on blood but are not known to science: vampires. In fact, nearly all cultures of the world have vampire mythoi—stories that tell of demons, monsters, ghosts, corpses, or other horrific beings that suck the blood from humans.

In Japan, for example, the *kappa*, which looks somewhat like a hairless monkey with fish scales, lurks in ponds and streams to grab unsuspecting passersby and suck out their blood. In Malaysia the *penanggalan* appears by day as an ordinary woman, but at night she can detach her head and fly about to look for victims with her stomach and entrails dangling from her severed neck. Her victims are new mothers and their infants, and she feeds on their blood with an invisible tongue. In ancient Greece vampiric demons would take on the appearance of a beautiful woman in order to lure young men to their deaths, whereas in ancient Rome vampiric demons sucked the blood of babies.

Corpse-Like Vampires

Beginning in the Middle Ages, Europeans spoke of demons entering disease-ridden corpses in order to make them rise from the grave to spread pestilence to people, animals, and crops. In some of these stories, the corpses merely contaminated their victims, perhaps after knocking on their doors.

But in others the corpses were vampires who preyed on their former neighbors or loved ones without warning.

During the eighteenth century in eastern Europe, stories of such vampire attacks resulted in waves of hysteria that led townspeople to dig up buried corpses and desecrate them to prevent any possibility of attacks. In writing of these incidents

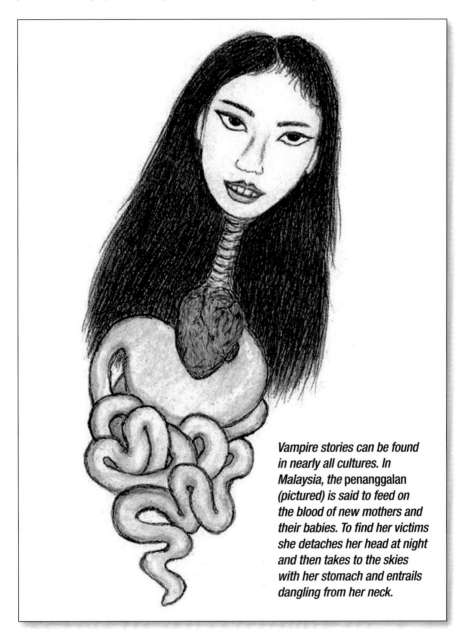

Vampire stories can be found in nearly all cultures. In Malaysia, the penanggalan (pictured) is said to feed on the blood of new mothers and their babies. To find her victims she detaches her head at night and then takes to the skies with her stomach and entrails dangling from her neck.

in his *Philosophical Dictionary* of 1764, the French philosopher Voltaire reported, "These vampires were corpses, who went out of their graves at night to suck the blood of the living, either at their throats or stomachs, after which they returned to their cemeteries. The persons so sucked waned, grew pale, and fell into consumption; while the sucking corpses grew fat, got rosy, and enjoyed an excellent appetite."[1]

Appearing Human

The notion that a vampire is a risen corpse still exists today in the Western world, but in the nineteenth century people began to speak of a different kind of vampire as well. This creature appears so like a living man that he can move among prospective victims—even those who are wealthy and powerful members of the nobility—with ease. (In the twentieth century people were able to envision female vampires of this nature too, but initially it was thought that only males could achieve this level of predation.) Typically suave and cultured, he is also able to charm and seduce humans, gaining their trust or perhaps mesmerizing them before going for the kill.

> "These vampires were corpses, who went out of their graves at night to suck the blood of the living."[1]
>
> —French philosopher Voltaire.

The idea that a vampire could convincingly masquerade as a human was introduced in the 1819 short story "The Vampyre" by John William Polidori. The vampire featured in this story, Lord Ruthven, marries the sister of an acquaintance and disappears after his bride is found dead—drained of her blood—on her wedding night. Adapted for the theater and opera, Polidori's work inspired several other authors to write stories featuring vampires of a similar nature.

Among the most influential of these works is the 1897 novel *Dracula* by Bram Stoker, which drew on Greek and southern Slavic folklore and vampire accounts from Romania and Transylvania. Stoker's title character, the vampire Dracula, is a wealthy Transylvanian count who is able to hypnotize his victims before biting their necks to drink their blood. He also has supernatural powers. As the character Abraham van Helsing, a Dutch professor who is also a vampire hunter, explains to those who want to fight Dracula:

> This vampire which is amongst us is of himself so strong in person as twenty men, he is of cunning more than mortal, for his cunning be the growth of ages . . . he is brute, and more than brute; he is devil in callous, and the heart of him is not; he can, within his range, direct the elements, the storm, the fog, the thunder; he can command all the meaner things, the rat, and the owl, and the bat, the moth, and the fox, and the wolf, he can grow and become small; and he can at times vanish and come unknown. How then are we to begin our strike to destroy him?[2]

Remorseful Vampires

In 1927 a play adaptation of the novel *Dracula* opened on Broadway and was wildly successful. Its lead actor, Bela Lugosi, subsequently starred in a film version of *Dracula* released in 1931, which was extremely popular. Lugosi's portrayal of Dracula quickly became the prevalent image of a vampire throughout the Western world.

Consequently, the majority of subsequent vampire novels, films, and television programs featured vampires who appeared to be living human beings, most of them cultured and wealthy. For example, in the 1976 best-selling novel *Interview with the Vampire* by Anne Rice, the vampire Louis begins his mortal life as the son of a rich plantation owner. When he is turned into a vampire against his will, he retains the style and decorum of the culture and wealth of his background.

However, Rice's vampire experiences feelings that the 1931 movie character Dracula never did. Louis feels remorse for satisfying his bloodlust; he considers it morally wrong to kill a human being, so he drinks the blood of animals instead. Eventually, however, he begins to feed on humans, while continuing to feel compassion for his victims and self-loathing because of his actions.

Bela Lugosi prepares to bite his sleeping victim in a scene from the 1931 movie Dracula. *Lugosi's portrayal of the vampire known as Count Dracula influenced writers and actors for years.*

Louis was not the first vampire in fiction to experience self-loathing. That distinction goes to Sir Francis Varney, the main character in the novel *Varney the Vampire; or, the Feast of Blood*, originally published in installments from 1845 to 1847. (The authorship of this story is unclear. Some ascribe it to Thomas Preskett Prest, others to his writing partner, James Malcolm Rymer.) Varney is so disgusted with himself that he commits suicide by throwing himself into a volcano. However, whereas Louis is said to be extremely attractive, Varney's victims shriek in terror when they see him. According to the story, Varney has a white, bloodless face, "dreadful" dark eyes, "fearful looking teeth . . . like those of some wild animal, hideously, glaringly white, and fang-like," and "long nails that literally appear to hang from the finger ends."[3]

Obscuring the Killer

In recent years vampires have increasingly been portrayed as being beautiful, sexy, and desirable. Perhaps the foremost example of such a vampire is Edward Cullen, a character in the 2005 novel *Twilight* and its sequels by Stephenie Meyer. Edward not only fights the urge to kill humans, but falls in love with one. After he and Bella Swan marry, Edward proves himself to be a compassionate, sensitive husband.

Vampires like Edward are becoming more common in modern literature and movies. As Mark Collins Jenkins, author of *Vampire Forensics: Uncovering the Origins of an Enduring Legend*, notes: "The vampire, who started life like [a] shambling zombie, has climbed the social ladder. Once the epitome of corruptible death, he has become a symbol of life—of life lived more intensely, more glamorously, and more wantonly, with bites having become kisses, than what passes for life on this side of the curtain [between life and death]."[4]

Although this image of caring vampires who live more vibrant lives than humans appeals to many modern readers and moviegoers, it does not appeal to those who believe that vampires once existed—and might still exist. Rather, their image of vampires reflects early written accounts of terror and helplessness. Based on these accounts, fear rather than desire should be the guiding emotion when contemplating encounters with vampires.

"This vampire which is amongst us is of himself so strong in person as twenty men, he is of cunning more than mortal, for his cunning be the growth of ages."[2]

—Bram Stoker's novel *Dracula*.

Fear, others contend, is precisely the response that has led to so many fanciful stories about vampires. To this way of thinking, fear fuels the imagination, and imagination has made vampires a convenient explanation for all manner of unexplainable events. But are these stories truly products of the imagination? Without proof one way or the other, who can say for certain that the many vampire stories from around the world and spanning so many centuries have no basis in fact? Until proof is found, many people will continue to question whether vampires once existed—and whether perhaps they still do.

Chapter 1

What Attributes Do Vampires Have?

"The best definition I can give of a vampire is a living, mischievous and murderous dead body. A living dead body!"

—J. Scoffern in his 1870 book, *Stray Leaves of Science and Folk-Lore*.
Quoted in Montague Summers, *The Vampire, His Kith and Kin*, Sacred Texts. www.sacred-texts.com.

"I go on, night after night. I feed on those who cross my path . . . I'm a spirit of preternatural flesh. Detached. Unchangeable. Empty."

—The vampire Louis, in the 1994 movie *Interview with the Vampire*.
Interview with the Vampire, directed by Neil Jordan. Burbank, CA: Geffen Pictures, 1994.

The most common beliefs regarding what vampires look like and how they behave largely originated with folklore and historical texts related to vampire attacks in the Western world. This is because writers of popular vampire novels and films most often relied on such sources in creating their characters. Consequently, when many people think of vampires, they visualize a physical being that resembles a human who is either living or recently deceased.

Physical Appearance

But even when vampires appear to be human, they still have some features that mark them as out of the ordinary. First and foremost, according to both European and North American folklore, they have fangs, which are sharp, long canine teeth. This is the case whether the vampire feeds by puncturing victims' skin or by tearing the flesh before sucking or drinking their blood. Either way, watching a vampire feed can be terrifying. As Aubrey Sherman reports in his book *Vampires: The Myths, Legends, & Lore*: "To actually see a vampire in whatever form encircle its prey in a frenzied attack or design a slow macabre courtship, then watch its fangs pierce exposed skin leaves a lasting impression."[5]

The skin of humanlike vampires is also unusual, because even though these creatures are flesh and blood, they are also the re-animated dead. In North American folklore this usually translates to skin that is as pale as the skin of the recently deceased—a

While descriptions vary, vampires are described in many accounts as having a resemblance to living humans. Common characteristics include pale skin, sharp fangs, and long fingernails.

Vampire Origin Myth

According to common belief, vampires are created by other vampires. But this has made people wonder where the very first vampire came from. Some say the answer can be found in a story that many believe dates back to around 450 BCE. In this story, an Italian named Ambrogio visits the Oracle of Delphi, a priestess in Greece who speaks for the sun god Apollo while delivering prophecies. While there Ambrogio falls in love with Selene, a maiden of the temple, and convinces her to leave the temple and marry him. This enrages Apollo, who curses Ambrogio so that sunlight burns him.

In trying to reverse this curse, Ambrogio receives other curses, gifts, and challenges from the gods. Specifically, he cannot stand the touch of silver, becomes immortal, has the great strength and fangs of a ferocious beast, and is not allowed to touch Selene. Nonetheless, he goes with Selene to the Greek city of Ephesus, where they live in a cave by day. There he realizes that his immortality means he will have to watch her age and die. He asks the goddess Artemis if she can change this, and the goddess allows him to touch Selene just once in order to drink her blood. Once her blood is within him, his blood can be used to bring immortality to others. As a result, Selene is restored as the goddess of the moon, and their children are born vampires just as Ambrogio has become.

condition that results once the heart stops pumping blood through the body. In European folklore, however, vampire skin is often described as ruddy, red tinged, or dark. This description probably applies to the vampire after he or she is sated with blood. For the same reason, according to European folklore, vampires typically appear bloated because they are engorged with blood.

Historical accounts also suggest that vampires have horrible breath and body odor. The description is understandable, considering these characteristics were mostly reported by people viewing the corpses of people suspected of being vampires. It also makes sense that such accounts would describe vampires as having long fingernails and hair. After death the skin retracts, which could make it appear as though hair and fingernails have continued to grow even after the body has been placed in a coffin.

Undisturbed Graves

Historical records also note that vampires have a remarkable ability to leave their graves without disturbing the soil. During the eighteenth century many scholars puzzled over how a vampire could manage this. One such scholar, a French abbot named Antoine Augustin Calmet, wrote in his 1746 book: "How a body covered with more than four or five feet of earth, having no room to move about and disengage itself, wrapped up in linen, covered with pitch, can make its way out, and come back upon the earth, and there occasion such effects as are related of it; and how after that it returns to its former state, and re-enters the underground . . . this is the question."[6]

Some people have theorized that the vampire's ability to do this is the result of the creature having supernatural powers. Those powers might include great strength and agility; highly acute senses of sight, hearing, and smell; and the ability to immobilize prey through hypnosis or psychic powers.

Spectral Appearance

The undisturbed graves might actually have another explanation. In some folktales, historical texts, and modern accounts, vampires are described as spectral rather than physical beings. These specters are most often ghostlike beings who bear a resemblance to the corpse to which they are somehow connected. Spectral vampires materialize in people's houses or elsewhere in order to feed on them or otherwise torment them.

Writer Henry More describes such a vampire as a walking corpse specter in his 1653 book *An Antidote Against Atheism*. The specter resembles a shoemaker in Poland who committed suicide and, according to More, later came back to terrify the living. More reports:

> Those [people] that were asleep it terrified with horrible visions, those that were waking it would strike, pull or press, lying heavily upon them like an ephialtes [nightmare] so that there were perpetuall complaints every morning of their last nights rest, through the whole town. . . . For this terrible apparition would sometimes cast itself upon the midst of their beds, would lie close to them, would miserably suffocate them and would so strike them and pinch them that not only blue marks but plain impressions of his fingers would be upon sundry parts of their bodies in the morning.[7]

The fact that this vampire did not suck the blood of his victims is not unusual. Many reports speak of spectral vampires draining the life force rather than the blood of their victims. Writer Konstantinos explains how this type of feeding can sustain walking corpse specters as well as how their existence relates to the puzzle of the undisturbed graves. He reports: "The general occult theory on the spectral type of vampire that thrived in folklore is that the spirit fed on either blood or energy (or both) by night, and by day returned to the corpse to infuse it with this energy. That would explain how a vampire could come up from its coffin without disturbing the soil—it could simply move through the ground in its astral body."[8]

Believers in the existence of an astral body say that it is a being's second body, is made of an unknown substance, and can leave the physical body to travel wherever it wishes. The astral body typically resembles the being to whom it belongs. However, it can also allow a spectral vampire to shape-shift, either to a different spectral form or to a material one.

Those who claim to have witnessed such remarkable events say that these changes in appearance most often happen right

According to some tales, vampires can transform themselves into other creatures. Among the most common ones cited are the vampire bat (pictured), and rats, cats, and wolves.

before the vampire attacks. In these instances a spectral vampire might levitate to attack the victim from above and then fly away. The spectral vampire might also appear throughout the encounter as a dark mass, a ball of light, mist, or some other indefinable entity. Like spectral vampires, physical vampires might also have the ability to transform themselves. But unlike spectral vampires, when physical vampires transform into other beings, they typically turn into nighttime predators such as vampire bats, rats, cats, and wolves.

Creating New Vampires

There is another difference between spectral vampires and physical vampires: Spectral vampires do not have the ability to reproduce. In contrast, physical vampires are often portrayed in folktales and other stories as having a powerful need to ensure the continued existence of their kind. In some accounts they actually mate with humans and produce offspring. More often, however, vampires turn living humans into vampires by draining the person's blood a little at a time, perhaps over days, until the victim dies and then becomes one of the undead. Sometimes this transformative process is also said to require the victim to drink some of the vampire's blood.

Vampires are not always made by other vampires, though. In many stories, events before or after death resulted in the transformation from human to vampire. Long ago, in some societies people believed that how a person died determined whether that person was in danger of becoming a vampire. For example, people who committed suicide or were violently murdered were considered to be at risk of becoming vampires. The same risk was also thought to apply to unrepentant sinners, children born with teeth, unbaptized infants, and anyone who had been cursed by a witch. Others at risk included people who were buried in an incorrect or unconventional manner (including those who had been denied proper burial rites) and corpses that had the misfortune of having a cat jump over them.

How a vampire is created is obviously a lot more complex than one might expect. It is difficult to know which of these ways is more common or more likely. As Katherine Ramsland says in her book *The Science of Vampires*, "There appears to be no consensus about how a vampire gets made, either in folklore or in fiction."[9]

> "There appears to be no consensus about how a vampire gets made, either in folklore or in fiction."[9]
>
> —*Katherine Ramsland in her book* The Science of Vampires.

Warding Off the Undead

Folklore also addresses the issue of how to prevent people from becoming vampires. But here, too, there is no consensus regarding the best means of protection, and the methods vary widely. Some methods relate to simply keeping a vampire from wanting or being able to go near a potential victim. Many of these involve the use of apotropaic items, which are places or objects believed to ward off the undead or other forms of evil. For example, in many traditions, vampires are unable to step on consecrated ground, which is ground that has been made sacred through religious ritual. Some traditions also hold that vampires cannot enter a home unless invited.

In popular literature and films, vampires are also said to avoid mirrors because, presumably, they have no reflection. This aversion is rarely mentioned in folklore. When it is, it is said that placing the mirror on a door will prevent the vampire from entering.

Other examples of apotropaic items that are objects include mustard seeds, branches of wild rose and hawthorn, and garlic. Garlic has long been believed to have demon-repelling powers. This belief is particularly strong in Romania and southern Slavic countries, whose folklore provided many of the vampire-related details in Bram Stoker's *Dracula*.

Even in modern times, people in these regions sometimes distribute garlic during church services. A person who tries to avoid the garlic might be suspected of being a vampire. A corpse suspected of being a vampire or being on the verge of becoming a vampire might have garlic placed in its mouth to keep demons away. In addition, animals are sometimes rubbed with garlic liniments to protect them from vampire attacks during the night.

The protective power of garlic also appears in vampire folklore from China, Mexico, and South America. In South America, for example, some people place garlic outside their windows and doors or wear it around their necks as protection against the bloodsucking *asema*. This creature is a spectral vampire who lives as an ordinary old man or woman by day but by night removes its skin, turns into a ball of light, and visits homes looking for victims.

Preventive Practices

Another method of protecting oneself and one's family from *asema* attacks involves scattering rice or sesame seeds on the ground outside the front door of one's house. The vampire is said to be unable to resist the urge to pick up each grain or seed. The hope is that this task will take so much time that the vampire will be caught outside at dawn and thus be killed by exposure to sunlight. To make doubly sure the vampire does not complete the task before sunrise, some people put a nail in with the seeds. If the vampire pricks its finger on the nail, the thinking goes, it would be startled into dropping the seeds and have to start all over. In other folklore, vampires are not only compelled to pick up such objects but to count them, so people scatter them on the graves of suspected vampires in order to keep them busy throughout the night.

Brandishing a holy object is also believed to drive away vampires. This has its basis in certain religious teachings that describe vampires as demons or the devil, or perhaps corpses possessed by one of these entities. Consequently, a crucifix, which is a Christian cross with the image of Jesus on it, is believed to be a powerful tool in warding off a vampire. In addition, because some crucifixes are made of silver, many people believe that silver drives away vampires as well. The same can be said of the holy water used in Catholic rituals. Some folklore suggests that vampires also cannot cross certain bodies of water, perhaps because water is a symbol of purity.

In some parts of the world, centuries ago, people also tried to prevent contact with a vampire by making corpses unable to walk among the living. For example, the newly deceased might be buried upside down to ensure that they would be unable to rise if the devil took possession of them. Similarly, they might be buried with their tendons severed so they could not walk. Alternatively, corpses might be buried with weapons or holy relics intended to frighten the demon away. In places where people believed that individuals became vampires not because of a demon but because they wanted to be vampires, corpses might be buried with items that would instead make them want to stay in their graves.

Killing Vampires

Corpses might also be buried with items that would kill the vampire if it attempted to rise, or at least make it harmless. As an example, science writer and microbiologist Alex B. Berezow points to discoveries made during an ongoing archaeological dig in a

The *Tlahuelpuchi*

In some parts of the world, vampirism is connected to witchcraft, often because witches are considered demon worshippers. This is the case, for example, in Latin America, where even today people in rural communities believe in a bloodsucking witch called the *tlahuelpuchi*. The *tlahuelpuchi* is a person, most typically a woman, who can transform herself into an animal like a turkey, dog, cat, or flea so she can move through a village unnoticed. Some people, however, are able to tell that an animal is actually a *tlahuelpuchi* because they are able to see the slight glow it emanates. The *tlahuelpuchi* also has hypnotic powers that enable her to convince people to kill themselves, typically by jumping from a great height to their death. She prefers the blood of babies, so parents who believe in her existence hang garlic and onions around their baby's cradle, two things said to repel the *tlahuelpuchi*. Garlic wrapped in a tortilla might also be placed within the baby's clothing.

graveyard in Drawsko Pomorskie, Poland. Six of the 285 graves at the site have provided evidence that in the 1600s and 1700s, "a suspected vampire was buried with a sickle across his body and/or a stone in his mouth," Berezow reports. "If the undead was to attempt a nightly prowl, the sickle would disembowel or decapitate him; if that didn't work, the stone would prevent him from biting anybody. Problem solved."[10]

Other cultures had other ways of trying to kill a corpse-like vampire before it could prey on the living. One of the most common methods was to destroy the corpse by burning it. Sometimes this was done only after the body was cut into pieces. In a five-volume history of England between 1066 and 1198, twelfth-century historian William of Newburgh writes of one such incident. It took place in Berwick, England, and involved a wealthy man who apparently rose from his grave at night and wandered through the town before returning to his grave before dawn. Afraid that the corpse would spread disease or start attacking people, the townspeople decided to take action. William reports:

> They, therefore, procured ten young men renowned for boldness, who were to dig up the horrible carcass, and, having cut it limb from limb, reduce it into food and fuel for the flames. When this was done, the commotion ceased. Moreover, it is stated that the monster, while it was being borne about (as it is said) by Satan, had told certain persons whom it had by chance encountered, that as long as it remained unburned the people should have no peace. Being burnt, tranquility appeared to be restored to them; but a pestilence, which arose in consequence, carried off the greater portion of them.[11]

William does not say why this pestilence occurred, although he implies it is the devil's work. However, in other cases in which burning a corpse was followed by disease, people said it was because the corpse had not been handled properly. Specifically, many believed that if the corpse's heart was not removed prior to burning, then the burning would not be successful.

Sunlight and Stakes

Similar to the belief that burning a corpse could destroy the vampire within, some people believe that a vampire will burst into flames upon exposure to sunlight. In works of fiction, such exposure is a common means of killing vampires. It is also a common way for vampires to kill themselves. Popular belief holds that vampires cannot die by their own hand—and because they are neither living nor dead, vampires also cannot die from old age or disease. Exposure to sunlight, therefore, provides one possible means of escape for vampires who do not wish for immortality.

However, killing vampires via sunlight exposure is rare in folklore, compared to more ordinary means of death. In the Balkans, for example, vampires can be shot or drowned. In other places decapitation is the preferred method. However, the most com-

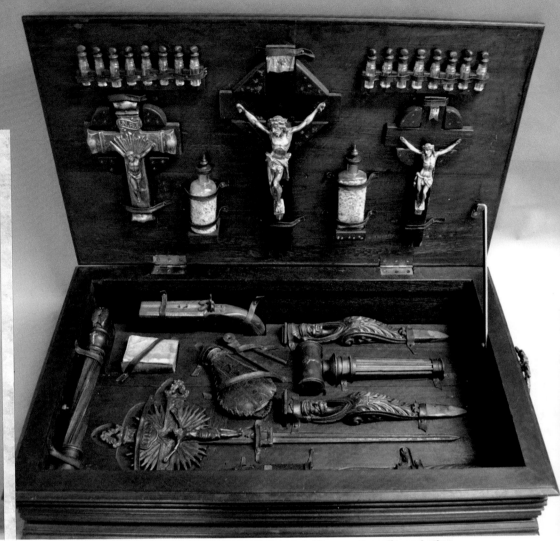

A vampire killing kit contains wooden stakes, crucifixes, salt, garlic, and other items once used by vampire hunters. In many tales, the favored method of killing vampires involves driving a stake through the heart, stomach, or mouth.

mon way to kill a vampire is to drive a stake through its heart, stomach, or mouth. Experts believe that this method developed out of the practice of driving a stake through a corpse in order to prevent it from being able to rise up out of its grave. This was done before the use of coffins became commonplace (that is, before the seventeenth century).

Historically, people have believed that the stakes used to kill vampires cannot be made from just any old piece of wood. Folktales from certain parts of the world specify that ash or oak must be used, whereas folktales from other regions might cite aspen, juniper, or hawthorn. And in Romania the killing of a vampire was said to require steel or iron stakes or long needles rather than wooden stakes.

Folklore has also spelled out the proper procedure for staking a vampire. In many Russian stories, for example, upon opening up the coffin of a suspected vampire, the staking had to be accomplished with one strong blow. Otherwise the vampire might rise up to attack.

Accounts from various places tell of stakings gone wrong. One such story, reported by Charles Ferdinand de Schertz in his 1706 *Magia Posthuma*, involves a shepherd in Bohemia. After the man's death, his corpse continued to rise from his grave and strangle people to death. Consequently, some townspeople opened the grave and staked the corpse, whereupon it thanked them for giving it a stick for fighting off wild dogs. That night the corpse rose again despite the stake and killed more people before morning than he had ever done before. The townspeople therefore pounded another stake into the corpse, hoping to end its nighttime forays. According to de Schertz's account, at the moment of impact they heard the corpse cry out and saw it bleed. They then burned the corpse, and the attacks finally stopped.

> "The . . . Church sexton sprinkled garlic on the remains and drove a stake through its heart, whereupon a dreadful scream issued from the body and blood gushed forth."[12]
>
> —*Eighteenth-century Austrian army surgeon Johann Flückinger.*

This is not the only occasion in which people reported hearing a cry or seeing blood after driving a stake into a corpse. Other reports from the eighteenth century also tell of corpses doing this upon being staked. An example of this appears in a report by Austrian army surgeon Johann Flückinger titled *Visum et Repertum* ("Seen and Discovered"). Specifically, in Serbia army officers dug up the corpse of a person who was suspected of being a vampire and responsible for the deaths of four people. Flückinger says: "The body had moved to one side in its grave, its jaws were open, and blood was trickling from its mouth. The officers and the Church sexton sprinkled garlic on the remains and drove a stake through its heart, whereupon a dreadful scream issued from the body and blood gushed forth."[12]

Living Vampires

Many of the historical writings related to vampires deal with how to kill these creatures. But in folklore there are also stories of vampires being captured and cured of their vampirism, whether temporarily or permanently. In the case of the latter, some go on to live relatively normal lives as humans.

In parts of eastern Europe, there are also vampires with human spirits. Known as *strigoi* (a plural noun, with the singular being *strigo*), after death they start off as poltergeists—invisible ghosts that torment former loved ones by pinching them, throwing things at them, and otherwise causing chaos through displays of physical energy. Then they become visible representations of the people they were in life. At first they merely continue to cause mischief. Soon, however, they turn into full-fledged vampires who suck the blood of their victims.

For the first seven years of this existence, the *strigo* has to return to its grave to rest in between attacks. After this period—if no one desecrates its body in the meantime—it is able to stop returning to its grave, which means it is free to go wherever it likes. And because it looks as human as it did in life, it can establish itself in a town where no one knows it is one of the undead.

In addition to undead strigoi—or *strigoi mort*—eastern European folklore speaks of another type of strigoi known as *strigoi viu*, or living strigoi. These are people born with some sort of defect or stigma that marks them as cursed to become a *strigo mort* after they die, and if they have any children, those children are also cursed to become strigoi mort after death. However, whereas centuries ago people firmly believed in such curses, today they generally reject them as nothing more than a way to ostracize certain individuals from society.

In fact, people today are far more likely than their ancestors to reject any suggestion that a human can become a vampire. According to polls, only 4 percent of Americans believe that vampires are real. Nonetheless, believers continue to argue that there are too many vampire stories from around the world to dismiss them all as complete fabrications. Many of these stories provide a wealth of details about what vampires are, how they act, and even how to kill them. Indeed, this level of detail makes it difficult for those who are unsure about their vampire beliefs to decide whether there is any truth to their existence.

Chapter 2

Why Do People Believe in Vampires?

"The folklore of the vampire has only a slight connection with the fiction, much the way the folklore of ghosts has little to do with the movie Ghostbusters.*"*

—Historian and folklorist Paul Barber.

Paul Barber, "Staking Claims: The Vampires of Folklore and Fiction," *Skeptical Inquirer*, March/April 1996. www.csicop.org.

"Vampires say a lot about our fears and hopes."

—Nina Auerbach, author.

Quoted in Ralph Blumenthal, "A Fear of Vampires Can Mask a Fear of Something Much Worse," *New York Times*, December 29, 2002. www.nytimes.com.

Since the beginning of human history, people have feared being attacked by predators in the dead of night. In ancient times they believed that these predators included blood-sucking monsters. More specifically, ancient Persians, Babylonians, Hebrews, Romans, and Greeks all believed in demons that attacked people to consume their blood. Ancient Persian artwork, for example, shows a man struggling to free himself from a monster attempting to suck his blood. And the epic Babylonian story of Gilgamesh, dating back to about 2000 BCE, describes a vampire-like creature called the Ekimmu.

Spiritual Beliefs

The Ekimmu is also an early example of the belief that vampires are a bridge between the living and the dead because the creature is said to be the spirit of someone who has died. Its victims are targeted because of some sort of psychic connection the Ekimmu formed with a person in life. This connection leads the Ekimmu to walk through walls to enter its victim's dwelling, whereupon it kills many or all of the people present.

In his book *The Devils and Evil Spirits of Babylonia*, Reginald Campbell Thompson provides a description of such a being by quoting a translation of a Babylonian prayer:

Spirits that minish [diminish] the land, of giant strength

Ghosts that break through houses . . .

Demons that have no shame

Knowing no mercy, they can rage against mankind.

They spill their blood like rain, devouring their flesh and sucking their veins.

They are the demons of full violence, ceaselessly devouring blood.[13]

That the Babylonian vampire was spoken of in a prayer is not unusual. The vampire has long been associated with religion. In fact, in many cultures people who went against their religious beliefs and/or refused to take part in rituals were believed to be at greater risk of becoming one of the undead. Similarly, some Christians believed that if a baby died before it was baptized, it would become a vampire.

This is the case in Bulgarian folklore, for example, which tells of unbaptized babies who were born on a Saturday becoming invisible vampires called *ustrels* after death. This transformation takes place nine days after burial, when the ustrel scrabbles out of its grave, seeks out a herd of cattle, and drinks the blood of the fattest cow or bull. Once the ustrel is sated, it returns to its grave to rest. The next day it takes up residence with the herd, living on the hind legs of a cow or the horns of a bull and continuing to feed on the herd as one by one the cattle weaken and die.

Unexplained Deaths

Stories about creatures like the ustrel typically arise out of efforts to explain the unexplainable. In times past, when an animal or human died for no apparent reason, people often wondered whether a supernatural or demonic cause was to blame. Similarly, in the days before modern medicine, individuals who found themselves feeling inexplicably ill suspected a vampire was the cause. John

In the days before modern medicine, sudden fatal illnesses were sometimes blamed on vampires. The bloodsucking creatures were thought to rise from their graves at night to attack and kill sleeping people.

Heinrich Zopfius reports on these suspicions in his 1733 *Dissertation on Serbian Vampires*, saying:

> Vampires issue forth from their graves in the night, attack people sleeping quietly in their beds, suck out all the blood from their bodies and destroy them. . . . Those who are under the fatal malignity of their influence complain of suffocation and a total deficiency of spirits, after which they soon expire. Some who, when at the point of death, have been asked if they can tell what is causing their decease, reply that such and such persons, lately dead, have risen from the tomb to torment and torture them.[14]

Experts believe that the idea that an inexplicable illness might be the fault of a vampire is why Europeans' belief in vampires became stronger during times of epidemics. Bioarchaeologist Lesley Gregoricka, who has excavated the graves of suspected vampires, says: "Today we might find it silly to believe in vampires . . . [but] before scientific understanding of contagion . . . vampires were perceived as a very real threat and represented one way of explaining the unexplainable."[15]

One disease that was commonly blamed on vampires is tuberculosis, also known as consumption. Without treatment, people with this disease gradually waste away. As the body weakens, it might look like the ill person is being drained of blood little by little over days, months, or even years. During this time their eyes become sunken and their nails appear longer because of the loss of fat and flesh, their breath becomes foul, and sometimes they cough up bloody sputum. Some also complain that it feels like a person is sitting on their chest. These symptoms so mimicked people's idea of a vampire attack that folklorist Michael E. Bell says, "The medical profession's failure to understand and successfully treat tubercu-

"Today we might find it silly to believe in vampires . . . [but] before scientific understanding of contagion . . . vampires were perceived as a very real threat and represented one way of explaining the unexplainable."[15]

—*Bioarchaeologist Lesley Gregoricka.*

losis prior to the twentieth century nourished the belief in vampires."[16] (The actual cause of the disease—bacteria transmitted via airborne particles—was not discovered until 1882.)

Exhumations

In some places the belief that consumption was somehow caused by vampires was so strong that if several people in a family or village died from the disease, the body of the first person to have contracted it was exhumed and examined for signs that it was a vampire. In eighteenth-century America particular attention was paid to the heart and lungs during this examination, in order to determine whether they contained liquid blood. The presence of this fluid was believed to mean either that reanimation had interrupted the decaying process or that the corpse had recently fed on the living. In either case it was considered proof of vampirism.

An example of this can be found in the exhumation of a suspected vampire in Belchertown, Massachusetts, in 1788. At that time the town minister, Justus Forward, became concerned that his deceased mother-in-law had become a vampire and was feeding on other family members, many of whom were ill with consumption. He arranged for her grave to be opened and discovered that her corpse seemed to have decayed normally. As a result, one of the witnesses suggested that they might have exhumed the wrong body.

Forward next exhumed the body of his married daughter, Martha Dwight, whose death had occurred almost six years earlier. This corpse appeared more lifelike, so its organs were removed and examined to determine whether they held liquid blood. Forward reports that in the case of his daughter, "the lungs were not dissolved, but had blood in them, though not fresh, but clotted." Moreover, "the lungs did not appear as we would suppose they would in a body just dead, but far nearer a state of soundness than could be expected. The liver, I am told, was as sound as the lungs." The assembled witnesses concluded that this was the vampire, so they "put the lungs and liver in a separate box, and buried it in the same grave, ten inches or a foot, above the coffin,"[17] a common means in America of preventing the vampire's rise.

But what those assembled did not know was that it is not shocking for liquid blood to be in the organs of a corpse. As historian and folklorist Paul Barber explains, blood does coagulate, or change to a solid, after death. However, "depending on how death occurred, it either remains coagulated or liquifies once again."[18]

Prior to the nineteenth century, many people also did not know that a body in a buried coffin decays much more slowly than does a dead animal aboveground. Therefore, they were surprised to see such corpses still looking relatively well preserved long after burial. In fact, gases within the body can cause it to expand to the point that it looks healthily plump. These gases can also force blood from the nose and mouth, making it appear as through the corpse has just fed on blood. And if a stake is driven through the corpse, escaping gases can make it sound as though it is screaming.

Moving Corpses

Such sights and sounds did much to convince people that vampires were indeed real. So, too, did cases in which people who had seemed dead before burial appeared to have come back to life. This sometimes occurred with victims of a disease called cholera. Although it kills fairly quickly, cholera can make its victims look like walking corpses—with pale, withered faces and glazed eyes. During the Middle Ages this resemblance to corpses sometimes led to premature burials. In the event the grave was reopened, possibly to check the corpse for signs of a vampire or to add more bodies, the person who had been buried prematurely

During the height of the Black Death in England in the 1300s, a body is dropped into a mass grave. People who appeared to be dead were sometimes buried along with the truly dead—and any sign of movement might be taken as evidence of a vampire.

might still be moving. To frightened onlookers it would seem obvious that the buried corpse had become a vampire.

Another disease, a plague known as the Black Death, was similarly associated with vampirism. The plague is caused by rat fleas (specifically, by a bacterium that can be transmitted into the bloodstream through their bite). This illness often causes victims to vomit blood. It also produces large, bulbous tumors—most commonly on the neck—that bleed when opened. The disease is so deadly that it killed millions in Europe, the Middle East, and parts of Asia during the fourteenth century and sometimes recurred in parts of Europe until the nineteenth century. In the sixteenth century, for example, an outbreak occurred in Italy, where the Venetian notary Rocco Benedetti wrote: "Workers collected the dead and threw them in graves all day without a break. Often the dying ones and the ones too sick to move or talk were taken for dead and thrown on the piled corpses."[19]

As with cholera victims, this means that someone decreed dead could later be found moving. This might explain why modern excavations of plague victim burial sites have uncovered staked and dismembered corpses. Moreover, because of the large number of deaths, victims were often buried in communal graves that had to be reopened periodically to add more corpses. This meant ample opportunity for noticing those unfortunate souls who had been buried alive—or, to the average person, a terrifying encounter with the undead.

Arnold Paole

Opening a gravesite, whether for an exhumation or to add more bodies, was unpleasant at best. At worst, it could trigger widespread vampire hysteria. Such was the case in Serbia in the eighteenth century, when townspeople threatened to abandon their entire village if authorities did not do something to stop the vampires in their midst.

The incident that triggered this hysteria is one of the best documented and most famous vampire exhumation cases in history. It involved a *hajduk*, or freedom fighter, named Arnold Paole, who claimed that while he was in Greece in about 1720, he had been visited by a vampire. He also contended that he had thwarted more vampire attacks by eating dirt from the vampire's grave and smearing its blood on his body.

Paole died around 1725 after falling off a hay wagon and breaking his neck. After his death, four people in the village claimed that Paole had become a vampire and was tormenting them. Within a month all four were dead, and villagers found evidence of livestock being attacked as well. Consequently, Paole's body was exhumed and examined.

Officials who documented the results of the exhumation said that the body had not decomposed as much as would be expected. They also reported fresh blood flowing from his eyes, nose, ears, and mouth as well as blood on his clothes, wrappings, and elsewhere inside of the coffin. Thinking all of these signs were proof of a vampire in their midst, the officials drove a stake through the body's heart—whereupon the corpse moaned and bled. This was considered further proof of the presence of a vampire. The officials burned the body and then did the same with the bodies of Paole's supposed victims.

From this point on, for several years no more vampire sightings took place. However, in 1731 suspicious deaths started to occur again. Over the course of three months, seventeen seemingly healthy people died—most after a short illness. The villagers attributed the deaths to meat eaten by one of the dead. The meat had apparently come from a sheep that had been killed during the first bout of vampire attacks. Fearing a new round of attacks, the villagers asked the military for help. Military authorities responded by exhuming the bodies, whereupon they discovered that twelve looked plump and flushed with blood. These corpses were deemed to be vampires; their heads were cut off, their heads and bodies burned, and their ashes thrown in a river.

Scholarly Debates

Between 1718 and 1734 there were several such incidents in eastern Europe. Panicked reports of vampire attacks spread

Sanguivoriphobia

An irrational fear of vampires is called sanguivoriphobia, a word that means "fear of blood eaters." People with sanguivoriphobia can suffer from panic attacks if they see anything that reminds them of vampires, including innocuous things like a child in a vampire costume. Many sufferers cannot even watch vampire movies, read books featuring vampires, or have a conversation about vampires without becoming extremely anxious. In severe cases people with sanguivoriphobia become convinced that many of the individuals they encounter in their daily lives are actually vampires, waiting for the right opportunity to attack unsuspecting humans. Some of these sufferers restrict their activities to daylight hours, believing that no vampire can go outside during that time. They might also barricade themselves into their homes at night, perhaps after surrounding themselves with items believed to ward off vampires, such as crucifixes and garlic.

from region to region, and corpses were increasingly dug up and destroyed. As with the Paole case, government officials were often involved in these incidents. In 1755, for instance, Empress Maria Theresa of Austria sent her personal physician, Gerard van Swieten, to investigate reports of vampire attacks in Moravia, a country then ruled by Austria. Ultimately, Van Swieten concluded that the reports were simply the result of superstition and a lack of understanding of the natural process of decay that takes place in the grave. Based on this conclusion, the empress banned the opening of graves and the desecration of bodies. This effectively ended vampire hysteria in eastern Europe.

However, by this time people in western Europe and America had heard of what was happening, and they feared vampire attacks on their own soil. Scholars debated whether this was possible, and some steadfastly refused to accept Van Swieten's position that vampires were not real. Others countered that if vampires were real, surely at least one of them would have been caught in the middle of an attack or some irrefutable physical evidence of their existence found.

In the mid-nineteenth century, a French spiritualist known as Dr. Pierart addressed this argument by expressing his belief in spectral vampires, who cannot physically be caught. He also insisted that not all of the many witnesses to vampire attacks could be wrong. He stated:

Nothing comes of nothing. Every belief, every custom, springs from facts and causes which give it birth. If one had never seen appear in the bosom of their families, in various countries, beings clothed in the appearance of departed ones known to them, sucking the blood of one or more persons, and if the deaths of the victims had not followed after such apparitions, the disinterment of corpses would not have taken place, and there would never have been the attestation of the otherwise incredible fact of persons buried for several years being found with the body soft and flexible, the eyes wide open, the complexion rosy, the mouth and nose full of blood and the blood flowing fully when the body was struck or wounded or the head cut off.[20]

Even skeptics admitted that the many witness statements related to vampire activities could not be dismissed out of hand. For example, French bishop Pierre Daniel Huet (1630–1721) wrote: "I will not examine whether the facts of vampirism, which are constantly being reported, are true, or the fruit of a popular error; but it is beyond doubt that they are testified to by so many able and trustworthy authors, and by so many *eye-witnesses*, that no one ought to decide the question without a good deal of caution."[21]

Manifestations of Fear

However, it is possible that these eyewitness reports were simply the product of imagination. Even during periods of rampant vampire corpse exhumations and desecration, scholars acknowledged that fear and hysteria can cause people to think they are being attacked by seen or unseen creatures when they are not. They also understood that the imagination can produce physical changes. As historian Koen Vermeir reports:

> In the seventeenth century, physicians and theologians did not dismiss vampirism as merely illusionary. Some scholars believed that vampires did not really exist, but they admitted that the overheated imagination of the alleged victims could have very real effects. These victims imagined that members of their family came back from the dead to prey on them, and this imagination could be so strong that many died as a result.[22]

Vermeir also reports that seventeenth-century scholars thought it was possible that the corpse's imagination was causing the vampire activity. He explains: "[Some] scholars believed in vampires in the sense that they considered the pernicious action that cadavers could exert on the living to be very real. They argued that the imagination of the corpse, still active because of the continuing operation of the vital powers, sent out noxious vapours or even a semi-corporeal avatar that could kill specific surviving relatives. In both cases the death of a victim of vampirism was interpreted as the very real result of the powers of the imagination, of the victim, or of the vampire-corpse respectively." But he adds that in the middle of the eighteenth century, "the perception of vampirism shifted from a 'disease of the imagination' to an 'imaginary disease.'"[23]

Modern Believers

Most people in the modern era would agree that vampires are products of imagination. But the belief in vampires has not dis-

A billboard in Serbia in 2012 warns drivers that a bloodsucking vampire is on the loose near the village of Zorazje. Officials urged villagers to carry garlic in their pockets and place wooden crosses in their houses.

appeared entirely. People who believe in vampires can still be found all over the world, and bouts of vampire hysteria occasionally crop up even today. For example, in the African country of Malawi beginning in 2003, people in some parts of the country abandoned their villages or refused to harvest crops because they feared that vampires were going to gradually drain them of blood. This fear has been fueled by rumors of vampires wielding hypodermic needles. Experts surmise that the vampire hysteria is tied to fears about the spread of AIDS in Africa. Another rumor, that the government has been working with vampires to provide blood to international agencies conducting medical research, has triggered incidents of civil unrest. Indeed, medical research related to AIDS has been conducted in Africa—but by humans, not vampires.

The belief in vampires, especially when it concerns people from long ago, is often described as resulting from fear, superstition, and ignorance. Because these ideas were so widespread, some modern believers view those fears and superstitions as an indication that vampires really did exist—and still do. In Konstantinos's book *Vampires: The Occult Truth*, Dante is a believer in the existence of vampires. In fact, he considers himself to be one. He has several vampire characteristics including being nocturnal and having teeth with sharp hooks on the tips, which makes it easier to pierce flesh. He does not know how or why he became a vampire, although he says, "I have theories, but only theories."[24]

Dante does not elaborate on those theories, but he confirms his belief that the vampire hysteria of centuries past was due not to unjustified fears, but to the activities of real vampires. He explains:

I offer this theory to link folklore and true vampirism: The corpses of the dead, no matter how evil in life, were, by definition, dead. Still, people were attacked, weakened, and even killed. . . . I submit that true vampires would watch a village until a likely candidate for mythic vampirism died. . . . Then, after the burial, the vampire would steal into homes, possibly dressed in clothes similar to what the dead person was buried in, and feed upon the villagers. When the suspected corpse was then dug up and staked, the vampire would simply move on to a new place and to fresh blood. And thus the vampire attacks would cease. In that manner, a single vampire could simulate an epidemic of vampirism in a very large area, going from village to village . . . thereby spreading the legend of the vampire.[25]

Although Dante admits that this is simply a theory, he is firm in his belief that vampires are real. Others are just as firm in their belief that vampires do not really exist. As skeptics point out, theories are nothing but speculation unless they can be proven. Absent such proof, believers and nonbelievers will always remain at odds over the validity of their convictions.

Chapter 3

Encounters with Vampires

"The stories told of these apparitions, and all distress caused by these supposed vampires, are totally without solid proof."

—Benedictine monk and scholar Antoine Augustin Calmet in his 1746 book, *Treatise on the Vampires of Hungary and the Surrounding Regions, or The Phantom World*.

Quoted in Matthew Beresford, *From Demons to Dracula: The Creation of the Modern Vampire Myth*. London: Reaktion, 2008, p. 15.

"If there ever was in the world a warranted and proven history, it is that of vampires: nothing is lacking, official reports, testimonials of persons of standing, of surgeons, of clergymen, of judges; the judicial evidence is all-embracing."

—Philosopher Jean-Jacques Rousseau in his "Letter to Christophe de Beaumont, Archbishop of Paris," 1763.

Quoted in James B. Twitchell, *The Living Dead: A Study of the Vampire in Romantic Literature*. Durham, NC: Duke University Press, 1981, p. 6.

When considering stories of vampire encounters, it is often difficult to determine which ones began as accounts the teller believed to be true and which ones began as tall tales invented to scare people. In fact, this task can be so difficult that Paul Barber says, "We will almost surely never know anything about the origins of the vampire lore."[26] In large part this is because much of this material dates back centuries; the circumstances of the origins have been lost, and the stories have likely been distorted over time.

The Vampire of Croglin Grange

Some small part of a vampire story originating in England in the 1800s, for instance, might be true. But it is also possible that many of the details were invented or embellished over time. This story, which takes place in a house known as Croglin Grange, appeared in clergyman Augustine Hare's multivolume autobiography *Story of My Life*. Hare presents the story as the recounting of a true event he heard about from an acquaintance, Edward Fisher-Rowe, on June 24, 1874.

The story concerns two men and their sister, who were renting Croglin Grange. One hot night while struggling to fall asleep, the woman looked through her bedroom window and noticed two tiny lights in a nearby churchyard. She was struck with terror when she realized that the lights were actually glowing eyes and that they were moving quickly toward the house. She rushed to her bedroom window and door to make sure they were locked. By this time the creature was scratching at the window, and she shrieked when she saw its shriveled brown face. Moments later a windowpane broke. The creature then reached its hand through the window to unlatch it, dashed into the room, grabbed the woman, and bit her throat as she screamed loudly. This brought her brothers to her aid, but by the time they arrived, she was lying unconscious in bed with her neck bleeding. One brother went to her side while the other looked out the window and saw a figure fleeing toward the churchyard.

> "We will almost surely never know anything about the origins of the vampire lore."[26]
>
> —*Folklorist Paul Barber.*

A doctor was then summoned. The woman regained consciousness, and her wound was bandaged. By this time those involved in the incident had concluded that the attacker was likely a madman escaped from a lunatic asylum. On the doctor's advice, the three siblings spent a few weeks in Switzerland to allow the woman to recuperate from her trauma. Once she had recovered, the woman and her brothers returned to Croglin Grange.

One night after their return, the mysterious figure again appeared at the woman's window after she had gone to bed. When she saw it she immediately called for her brothers. They

According to the story of England's Croglin Grange, a woman was bitten in the throat in the dead of night. She claimed that a hand reached through a broken pane to unlatch the window. The creature then stepped into the room and attacked her.

ran outside brandishing guns and shot at the creature. One shot struck its leg, but it still managed to reach the church-yard, where it vanished near a burial vault. Now the men sus-pected that the attacker was a vampire. The next morning they and some townspeople looked at the corpses in the vault and discovered that one of them not only had a brown, shriveled face but showed evidence of having been shot in the leg. They burned the corpse, and there were no further attacks.

Evaluating the Story

The story of the Croglin Grange vampire has been examined several times over the years to see whether it could be a true account. In 1924 English author Charles G. Harper visited the supposed site of the house, in the town of Cumberland. There he found a two-story house named Croglin Hall but could not find the one-story house called Croglin Grange that Hare had described in his story. (However, by definition, a grange is simply a country house with farm buildings attached.) Harper also found no church or burial vault in the area. He therefore concluded that the entire story had been fabricated.

Nonetheless, in the early 1960s author Francis Clive-Ross decided to conduct his own investigation into the circumstances of the story. Local residents told him that the tale of the vampire of Croglin Grange was first told between 1680 and 1690 by a member of the family who owned the house. At that time Croglin Hall was a one-story house (a level was added around 1720), which means that it once fit the description of the story's Croglin Grange. Moreover, a chapel was nearby, and when Clive-Ross discovered its foundation stones, he felt it likely that a burial vault once existed near the house. Consequently, he concluded that the story had at least some basis in fact.

In 1968, five years after Clive-Ross published a book about his findings, another author, parapsychologist David Scott Rogo, did his own research into the matter. He uncovered material that suggests that the story of Croglin Grange might have existed around the same time as the 1847 novel *Varney the Vampire*. He believes the two stories might have been penned by the same person as a fictional work.

However, Rogo's theory ignores the possibility that the author of the Varney story might have known of and drawn from the Croglin Grange story in producing his work. It also does not take into account Clive-Ross's position that the Croglin Grange story existed nearly two hundred years earlier than the publication of the Varney story—a position that paranormal investigator Lionel Fanthorpe confirmed in March 2011 after visiting the site of Croglin Hall and its nearby church. But Fanthorpe says that even if these things are true, it is possible that the creature that attacked the woman at Croglin Grange really was simply a madman escaped from an asylum. In this case perhaps the blood on the woman's neck was not from the bite, but from blood on the man's hands due to the broken window glass.

The Highgate Vampire

Given the murkiness of the Croglin Grange story's origins, people will likely never stop arguing over its veracity. As Konstantinos points out, this is not uncommon. He explains: "With retelling, stories often become a little more exciting than they might have been. Eventually, the original facts can be lost even by the storytellers, making some stories in folklore a little hard to accept as truth."[27] And if a story's circumstances involve a dark night and a scary location, it is even more likely that people will find the story hard to accept. This is because it is commonly believed that such circumstances produce a kind of fear that causes people to imagine monsters, ghosts, and similar strange beings.

> "With retelling, stories often become a little more exciting than they might have been."[27]
>
> —*Konstantinos in his book* Vampires: The Occult Truth.

This belief is the reason many dismiss the story of the ghost vampire of Highgate Cemetery in London, England. In 1967 two sixteen-year-old girls were walking past the run-down cemetery late at night when they thought they saw bodies emerging from some of the tombs and ran home frightened. A few weeks later, a couple walking the same route at night spotted a humanlike figure with a hideous face near the gate of the cemetery, hovering slightly above the ground. Others subsequently spotted the specter under similar circumstances. But not all agreed that it was a ghost. One witness, Brian Travis, described the creature by saying:

I'd estimate its height at between seven or eight feet. I'm five feet eight inches tall and it towered over me. It was enormous! It was neither solid nor transparent. My overall impression was that it was a black figure wearing dark garments which flowed and stirred in the wind—but there was no wind. The edges of what it was wearing were moving. No face. Where eyes would have been if it were human, there were just two red pits, red glows, and I was very conscious that it was looking at me. At that point I realised that I was up against an entity that was both powerful and malignant. It was radiating evil, that's the only way

I could describe it. This wasn't a ghost, this was an entity. There was nothing remotely human about it. It simply was not human. As an ex-Army Officer I'd come up against life threatening situations, but faced with that thing the fear was worse than anything you could imagine.[28]

Media reports about the supposedly haunted cemetery led to new, more grisly discoveries: several animal cadavers, drained of blood. Then the body of a person was found in a pool of blood caused by a deep throat wound. Soon the press was reporting

A ghostly vampire is said to haunt Highgate Cemetery in London (pictured). One person who claims to have seen the mysterious creature says it was very tall and glowed red where the eyes would normally be found.

Vampires Who Do Not Drink Blood

During the centuries when vampire hysteria was common, not all reanimated corpses deemed vampires were bloodsuckers. One such corpse was that of a shoemaker in the town of Breslau, Silesia (now Wroclaw, Poland). In September 1591 he committed suicide, but his relatives hid this fact so he could be buried in consecrated ground. Several weeks after his death, however, he began appearing as a ghost at people's bedsides in the night. Instead of sucking their blood, the ghost vampire would pinch, poke, and try to suffocate them. Sometimes his actions left bruises and finger impressions on their skin.

Finally, in April 1592 authorities dug up the corpse. (By this time they had learned that the shoemaker had killed himself and thought that reburying him under the town gallows, in unhallowed ground, would end his nightly attacks.) The corpse was intact, did not smell bad, had supple joints, and exhibited a rose-shaped mark—which many assumed was a magic symbol—on the big toe of the right foot. Therefore, many were not surprised when the attacks continued even after the reburial. Two weeks later the corpse was dug up again; its heart was removed; its arms, legs, and head were cut off; and all body parts were burned and the ashes thrown in a river. After that, the ghost vampire never appeared again.

that a vampire was on the loose in Highgate, and individuals began going into the cemetery at night to see if they could spot the creature. Peter Underwood, president of the Ghost Club Society and lifetime member of the Vampire Research Society, says:

Alleged sightings of a vampire-like creature—a grey spectre—lurking among the graves and tombstones have resulted in many vampire hunts. . . . In 1968, I heard first-hand evidence of such a sighting and my informant maintained that he and his companion had secreted themselves in one of the vaults and watched a dark figure flit among the catacombs and disappear into a huge vault from which the vampire . . . did not reappear. Subsequent search revealed no trace inside the vault but I was told that a trail of drops of blood stopped at an area of massive coffins which could have hidden a dozen vampires.[29]

As media attention to the story grew, there were calls to hunt down the vampire and kill it. On March 13, 1970, a mob of people showed up at the site—with garlic, crosses, holy water, and stakes—to do just that. The police tried and failed to control the resulting chaos, but despite overrunning the cemetery, the crowd found no supernatural being on the grounds that night.

More sightings were reported, as was one attack. In 1971 someone driving past the cemetery noticed a young girl on the ground fighting off an attacker. When the driver pulled over to help her, the attacker vanished without a trace. Later the girl described her assailant as a tall, humanlike figure with a pale face and supernatural strength.

On another occasion, a man who had become lost in the cemetery as darkness fell encountered a similar figure. He later said that the vampire so terrified him that he could not move until after it vanished right in front of him. Such sightings continued at Highgate until 1974, the same year that self-professed vampire hunter Seán Manchester claimed to have tracked down the vampire in the cemetery, staked it through the heart, and burned it.

A Popular Hunting Ground?

Some people say that Manchester was just taking credit for the end of a bout of vampire hysteria. They believe that the first few stories of vampire sightings were cases of susceptible individuals' eyes and imaginations playing tricks on them, and their stories then inspired others to see the creature, too. Then the media whipped the public into a frenzy over the vampire, and this encouraged still others to jump in with their own stories as a way to become a part of what was going on.

Other people, however, argue that there are too many sightings of the vampire for all of the accounts to be made up. They also note that the early stories, before the media frenzy began, provided similar details about the creature, even though the witnesses were not conferring with one another over these details. In addition, they point out that other vampires have been sighted in London as well, which means that it would not be unusual for Highgate to have one.

Indeed, a 2014 study found that at least 206 vampire encounters have been reported in the United Kingdom over the past one hundred years. This is more encounters than in Transylvania, the birthplace of the fictional vampire Dracula, which has only had nine or ten. In making this determination, the head of the study, paranormal investigator Lionel Fanthorpe, relied on historical archives, police reports, eyewitness accounts, and paranormal investigative records. The results surprised him. He says, "I really only expected to find one or two instances [of vampire encounters] in Britain. So I was amazed when I discovered one story after another. And I really didn't expect to find more here than in somewhere like Transylvania."[30]

Most of these cases involved vampires who more or less fit the classic description of a vampire—that is, a creature that looks human, though perhaps with odd features. For example, in the 1990s paranormal investigator Tom Robertson received reports that animal carcasses completely drained of blood had been found in the woods near Lochmaben Castle in Scotland. He went there to have a look around, and after about a half hour, he caught a fleeting glimpse of a figure. Wanting to know what it was, he decided to come back another day and spend the night there in his car. At the time, although he believed in the paranormal, he did not believe in vampires. That changed when he went for a walk after dark. He reports:

> "I really only expected to find one or two instances [of vampire encounters] in Britain. So I was amazed when I discovered one story after another."[30]
>
> —Paranormal investigator Lionel Fanthorpe, who has studied UK reports of vampire encounters.

I took my time walking up and down the paths then felt something—a presence, not spiritual but physical. I stopped but could hear no footsteps. A shiver passed over me. The hairs on my neck and arms stood on end. I turned slowly. And there it was . . . the most hideous sight—a walking, decomposing corpse. Its face was as grey as granite, its eyes as black as coal. The skin seemed transparent except for the purple veins protruding from the creature's dead, withered tissue. It was tall but round-shouldered and a hood was pulled over its head, dressed in sacking. . . . The creature suddenly took flight, springing up on to a branch and gliding from tree to tree like Tarzan on steroids.[31]

Murderers as Vampires

Robertson believed that this creature was a vampire and that it was living in the woods, feeding off rabbits and other forms of wildlife. Stories of modern-day vampire encounters typically feature creatures that live in remote or unpopulated areas—woods, cemeteries, abandoned castles, and the like—where they can kill isolated prey without being detected. However, some believers in vampires suspect that the creatures also operate in densely populated areas. There they make their kills look like the work of murderers who are entirely human, and they are able to cover their tracks to avoid detection and capture.

The prime example of this is Jack the Ripper, whose identity has never been discovered. (The name "Jack the Ripper" comes from a letter written to the police by someone claiming to be the murderer.) A serial killer operating in the Whitechapel district of London from 1888 to 1891, he murdered at least five people, and all of the victims had slashes at the throat. No one heard the victims scream, and no one ever caught the killer in the act.

People who believe the Ripper was a vampire say that the killer must have drunk blood from the victims' throat wounds. They also say that he must have hypnotized his victims prior to killing them so they would not scream. In addition, the fact that the killings stopped abruptly, just when police efforts to find the Ripper intensified, suggests to vampire believers that he simply relocated. Author Lynn Gibson theorizes that he went to Croglin Grange. She says:

> It is conceivable that Jack relocated to Croglin Grange, London as the case takes place from 1896–1900. . . . The description of this vampire was that of a browned and mummified creature, which would suggest that he had not fed regularly for some time. Having had to flee Whitechapel and re-establish himself into a new terrain could explain the lack of feeding.[32]

But none of this can be proved, and law enforcement experts familiar with the Ripper case say it is ridiculous to even suggest that he was a vampire.

Similar comments are made in regard to murderers whom some have dubbed living vampires. This term refers to mortal beings displaying vampiric tendencies. One of the most prominent examples of this is Elizabeth (or in her native tongue, Erzsébet) of Bathory, a sixteenth-century Transylvanian countess nicknamed the Blood Countess. Acting on suspicions that Elizabeth had abducted some noblemen's daughters, King Matthias II of Hungary and Croatia ordered Count Gyorgy Thurzo to pay an impromptu visit to her castle in Hungary. (There had long been rumors that she was abducting and killing peasant girls in the area, but because her family was rich, powerful, and highborn, these rumors were ignored until her actions affected the nobility.) Thurzo not only caught Elizabeth in the act of torturing young girls—she had a torture chamber dedicated to this purpose—but discovered the mutilated bodies of other victims.

As a result, she was arrested for murdering eighty people. However, at her trial—where more than three hundred witnesses, including survivors of her brutality, testified—she was accused of torturing and killing as many as 650 girls. She was found guilty and imprisoned until her death three years later. By this time it

Elizabeth of Bathory, a sixteenth-century countess from Transylvania, is said to have abducted and killed dozens of young women and then bathed in their blood. This ritual, she hoped, would keep her forever young.

was said that her motivation for the killings was that she believed if she drank and bathed in the blood of young maidens she would stay forever young. This craving for blood and its connection to immortality has led some people to call Elizabeth a vampire.

However, Matthew Zarzeczny, a writer for the website Top-Tenz, reports that although Elizabeth of Bathory's name typically lands on lists of the top ten real people alleged to be vampires, she might have been framed for the crimes. He suggests

Popular Stories

Stories of modern vampire encounters are often tales told by someone relating something that supposedly happened to a friend of a friend of a friend. These accounts are therefore unreliable, but their unreliability does not necessarily make vampire believers question their veracity. An example of such a story, which has been shared on various websites, involves a man who is hit by an ambulance in a busy intersection and thrown 30 or 40 feet (9 to 12 m). The ambulance then takes him to the hospital, where he refuses treatment and tries to leave. A nurse convinces him to wait in an examining room. A few minutes later she encounters a dead orderly sitting in a wheelchair with puncture marks on his neck. She screams, attracting a security guard, and as he arrives the mysterious man dashes past them both. The guard shoots at him, but although the man is struck by the bullets he is unharmed. He leaps out of a window to the ground twenty stories below and runs off.

she and her family had powerful enemies who might have fabricated evidence and testimony. He explains: "She was a powerful woman in a misogynistic time. She was also a Protestant whose primary political opponents were Catholics. Moreover, a supposed diary of hers has yet to be examined by historians. As such, the truth behind her legend is still not entirely clear. Yet, she continues to be depicted as a vampire killer in popular culture."[33]

A Negative Side Effect

Zarzeczny also warns that connecting real historical figures to vampirism can be damaging to society. He says: "Some of this almost obsession with vampires is fun and relatively harmless. On the other hand, it has also resulted in the depiction of historical figures in a less than historical manner and has encouraged mentally ill people to seriously believe they are either vampires or that they should at least act like them. As such, the vampire craze has had a negative side effect that blurs history and can even have fatal consequences."[34] Nonetheless, people continue to speculate on whether certain real mass murderers became killers because of a vampire encounter that tainted them somehow—whether by turning them into vampires or dooming them to become vampires after death.

Chapter 4

Can Science Explain the Belief in Vampires?

> "Most of these modern vampires are psychotic and have abandoned the traditions of their forebears. It is much more likely for your twentieth-century vampire to be a pallid-faced little man with a greasy tie and carpet slippers living in the suburbs than a Gothic monster."
>
> —Anthony Masters, author of *The Natural History of the Vampire.*
> Quoted in Tori E. Godfree, "Vampires: The Ever-Changing Face of Fear," *Student Pulse*, 2010. www.studentpulse.com.

> "It gets me really angry when people say that individuals who believe in vampires or think they themselves are vampires are crazy. I know that I am not crazy. In fact, I think I'm a pretty rational person. For that reason, I'm afraid to call myself a vampire, but I guess I'm a mortal one."
>
> —Megan, a self-professed vampire.
> Quoted in Konstantinos, *Vampires: The Occult Truth*. Woodbury, MN: Llewellyn, 2010, p. 85.

Many vampire encounters, some more believable than others, have been reported throughout history, but none has ever been proven real. People who are interested in finding out once and for all if vampires exist hope that science might be able to help answer this question. Specifically, they want scientists to determine whether there really are predatory creatures in human form that thrive on human blood, or, if vampires are not real, what else could explain the details provided in stories of vampire sightings and attacks.

Whether science can actually perform this role is debatable. At least one scientist, physics professor Costas Efthimiou, says that myths and folklore cannot be tested scientifically. He states: "These popular myths make for a lot of Halloween fun and great movies with special effects, but they just don't hold up to the strict tests of science."[35] When Efthimiou applies the principle of geometric progression to the question of whether vampires are real, he concludes that their existence is mathematically impossible. For the sake of illustration, Efthimiou assumes that the first vampire appeared at the beginning of the year 1600. Then, assuming that a vampire has to feed once a month (thereby turning a human into a vampire who would also need to feed), each month there would be double the number of vampires than the month before and the number of humans would decrease accordingly. In other words, in February there would be two vampires, in March four vampires, in April eight vampires, in May sixteen vampires, and so on until the end of the year, when there would be 4,096 vampires. Continuing this progression, using historical population estimates, Efthimiou calculated that all of the humans in the world would have become vampires within two and a half years.

> "These popular myths make for a lot of Halloween fun and great movies with special effects, but they just don't hold up to the strict tests of science."[35]
>
> —Physics professor Costas Efthimiou.

Reanimation and Immortality

Others, however, point out that no one knows how often vampires feed or whether every person they feed on necessarily becomes a vampire. Some also say that mathematics aside, scientific knowledge of the physical world has much to contribute to discussions of whether vampires exist. This is particularly true when it comes to fields of scientific study related to how organisms develop and function (such as biology, physiology, anatomy, and anthropology), how people perceive reality (physics and psychology), and crime-scene analysis (criminal forensics).

In regard to vampire physiology, many people have written about the reasons why vampire hunters who opened up coffins might have discovered corpses that seemed very much alive.

Long after death, in the right conditions, a human body can still look remarkably human—with skin, teeth, and even hair sometimes still visible. But to vampire hunters of the past, these features were a clear sign that they had found their prey.

Gases in the body can make a corpse look bloated and moan when staked. Skin changes make it seem like fingernails have continued to grow and that teeth are instead fangs. In addition, under certain soil or coffin conditions, corpses can continue to look lifelike for decades or even centuries.

Less attention has been paid, however, to research that suggests that it might be possible for a body to become reanimated. This possibility is based on the theory that certain emotions and repetitive actions can become imprinted on the body. According to forensic psychologist Katherine Ramsland, some in the scientific community are developing the theory that these "body memories" might remain after death. Moreover, she writes, "each organ in the body processes specific emotional energies, and even if the energy known as consciousness leaves the body at death and continues to exist, that does not negate how intricately linked it is to the body while in the physical realm. In other words, the 'soul' may depart but some residual structure of the personality could remain in the body tissues at a cellular level, along with the memories and manner of processing perceptions." Ramsland adds that if a person's personality resides in body tissue, "then the corpse still has the *potential* to be that same person."[36]

Another avenue of exploration is whether it would be possible for a vampire to have the kind of immortality described in folklore. Because all creatures—living and dead—are composed of cells, experiments related to animal and human longevity would also apply to vampires. According to Ramsland, "science appears to have found a way to make normal cells last a lot longer and perhaps even become immortal."[37] In theory, at least, this could help explain accounts of vampires as immortal beings.

Rabies

Other explanations for vampires might be found in the characteristics of certain diseases. Rabies has been cited as an example of a disease that could have been confused with the existence of vampires. Rabies, which results from the bite of an animal that carries the rabies virus, attacks the nervous system. If left untreated or if treatment is given too late, rabies can develop into a form of the disease called furious rabies. People afflicted with this form of the disease may be driven to biting other people. A study by Spanish neurologist Juan Gomez-Alonso found that almost 25 percent of men with untreated rabies were compelled to bite other people.

Furious rabies can produce other symptoms reminiscent of vampire qualities mentioned in folklore. Sufferers are prone to sneer, bare their teeth, and hiss like vicious beasts. They cannot stand drinking water even though they are incredibly thirsty. They exhibit a pronounced aversion to strong stimuli, like bright sunlight and the odor that garlic produces. In addition, because the virus is carried in saliva, if someone with rabies bites another person, that person is highly likely to become infected—just as the bite of a vampire is said to be able to turn someone into a vampire.

Given all these similarities between rabies sufferers and vampires, Gomez-Alonso decided to examine records of rabies outbreaks in eastern Europe during the eighteenth century, when there were also numerous reports of vampire epidemics. He discovered that rabies outbreaks were typically followed by accounts of vampire outbreaks—and this was during a time when the region was troubled by rabid wolves, dogs, and bats. Therefore, he believes that at least in eastern Europe, vampire stories were inspired by rabies attacks.

Porphyria

Other experts suggest a different disease for the possible source of vampire lore: porphyria. Porphyria is a rare genetic disorder that causes the body to have trouble making heme, which provides the red pigment in blood and is involved in the transportation of oxygen in the bloodstream. This disorder can make the skin so sensitive to sunlight that it can develop painful lesions. It can also cause gum deterioration that might make teeth look like fangs. In addition, without treatment some sufferers might feel compelled to drink blood, possibly because in large enough

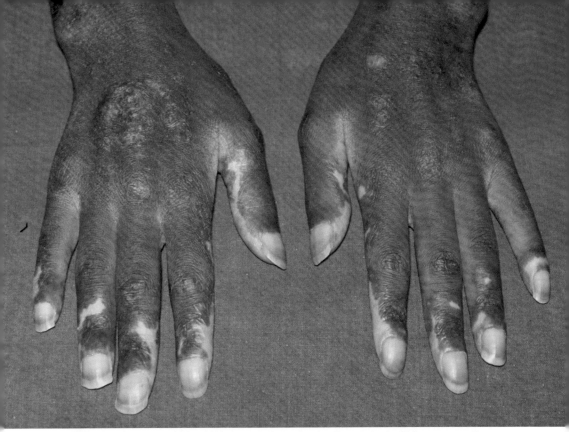

White patches are visible on the hands of a person with porphyria. This rare genetic disorder can cause skin color changes and sensitivity to sunlight—both of which are also said to be signs of a vampire.

amounts, heme can be absorbed into the bloodstream through the stomach wall.

According to historian Mark Collins Jenkins, there is yet another reason that porphyria might be the source of vampire stories. He reports:

> Too much garlic is known to destroy the functioning of heme in the liver. So a porphyria victim, believing himself prey to a vampire and therefore moved to surround himself with garlic, might by that very action inadvertently trigger the latent porphyria in his own loved ones (the disease runs in families). Once he died, and his relatives sickened in turn, it might look to all the world like the handiwork of vampires—the latter being widely supposed to prey on their next of kin.[38]

Vampire Viruses

For many years people have theorized that vampirism might be caused by a virus that is passed from a vampire to a nonvampire, perhaps during feeding, reproduction, or casual contact. Some of these theories suggest that a vampire virus somehow alters human DNA, a substance in cells that carries information on how a living being will look and act. Other theories concentrate on the means by which the virus developed. Some say it began naturally, whereas others say it was developed in a laboratory and either accidentally or intentionally released on an unsuspecting public. (Theories that involve intentional release often blame terrorists or government operatives, and in either case they typically speak of a government cover-up following the event.) Popular fiction has fueled these ideas through works such as Richard Matheson's novel *I Am Legend* and the movie series *Blade*. Both of these feature vampirism that is caused by a body-altering disease.

Genetic Mutations

Some people have speculated that genetic mutation, rather than disease, might be responsible for vampires—at least in a theoretical sense. Descriptions of the transformation from human to vampire are common in vampire lore. What if, during a vampire bite, some of the vampire's blood is transferred into the victim's body? Could this transfer genetic material from the vampire to the victim? And could this lead to changes in the victim's physiology?

Even scientists who do not believe in the existence of vampires say that it is possible to alter a being's traits via the transfer of genetic material. This can be done in a lab through genetic engineering, or it can occur as part of a natural process. In regard to the latter, Ramsland reports:

Overt manipulation [in the lab] . . . is not required for the body to inspire its own rearrangements and become something other than what it is. Sometimes it happens via what's called transposons or "selfish genes." They insert themselves into other chromosomes and thereby reorient the cellular process, causing mutation. Generally this happens on a small scale, but it could be these very genes that hold the key to the vampire transformation.[39]

Mental Illness

Ramsland is not saying that vampire transformations are real, only that they are scientifically possible. But she says that it is also possible for a transformation of the personality to be the reason someone adopts vampire-like behavior. Specifically, some individuals act like vampires because of a mental illness that she calls vampire personality disorder.

This illness has not been officially recognized as a mental disorder (a recognition that requires it to be listed in the *Diagnostic and Statistical Manual of Mental Disorders*, a guidebook for psychiatrists). Nonetheless, psychiatrists know that some people do suffer under the delusion that they either are a vampire or can become one. This belief causes them to adopt behaviors of vampires, such as drinking blood. Some commit gruesome murders as well.

Among the apparent sufferers of this illness is former art student Matthew Hardman from the Isle of Anglesey in the United Kingdom. At age seventeen, after becoming obsessed with vampires, he decided that drinking blood would make him immortal. Therefore, in November 2001 he killed his next-door neighbor, ninety-year-old widow Mabel Leyshon, and drank her blood from a saucepan.

At Hardman's trial, his lawyers argued that he had not committed the crime, and no testimony related to mental illness was offered. The judge bemoaned the absence of such expert testimony as he sentenced Hardman to a minimum of twelve years in prison, saying, "One might hope for a psychological explanation for your behaviour but none is offered." Nonetheless, the judge stated:

> I am drawn to the conclusion that vampirism had indeed become a near obsession with you, that you really did believe that this myth may be true, that you did think that you would achieve immortality by the drinking of another person's blood and you found this an irresistible attraction. . . . It may well seem incredible but in my judgment that is where the evidence leads.[40]

Blood Drinkers

A related illness, also not listed in the *Diagnostic and Statistical Manual of Mental Disorders* but known by psychiatrists since the nineteenth century, is clinical vampirism. An obsession with drinking blood, this illness today is more commonly known as Renfield syndrome. This name refers to a madman in the novel *Dracula* who serves Dracula and is obsessed with consuming living creatures in order to acquire their life force.

Someone with clinical vampirism might exhibit other characteristics of being a vampire in addition to drinking blood, but this is not necessarily the case. The illness has a sexual component, whereby the sufferer becomes excited by the act of drinking blood. The illness also has stages whereby the sufferer starts off cutting himself and consuming his own blood (sufferers are overwhelmingly male), then drinks animal blood and perhaps eats live animals. This is in addition to consuming human blood. In this last stage the individual might drink blood stolen from blood banks or directly from a living human. In the most severe cases, the person commits murder in order to obtain the blood.

Some people drink human blood for an altogether different reason: They simply want to emulate the vampire lifestyle. These people often rely on blood provided willingly by individuals who want to participate in the vampire lifestyle themselves. This alternate lifestyle typically reflects characterizations of vampire behavior, clothing, and hairstyles drawn from novels and movies. Some of the adherents to this lifestyle practice sanguinarian vampirism (which involves drinking blood to satisfy thirst rather than for sexual excitement), whereas others practice psychic vampirism (whereby people are said to feed off of each other's psychic energy).

Those who drink blood as part of the vampire lifestyle disagree over whether animal blood is a satisfactory substitute for human blood. Some say that human blood is more satisfying and gives them more energy than animal blood. Others say there is no difference between the two except perhaps for taste. However, according to science, the two are not equal. As the National Heart, Lung, and Blood Institute states: "There is no substitute for human blood. Human blood cannot be manufactured; animal blood cannot replace it. People are the only source of [human] blood."[41]

Experts also say that blood can be toxic to humans if it is consumed in large quantities. This is because blood is rich in iron; the human body does not easily excrete iron, and too much iron in the system can cause a host of serious health problems, including liver damage. Therefore, science-based paranormal investigator Benjamin Radford says: "Feel free to participate in the vampire craze and goth subcultures, but if you're thinking of sampling human blood, make sure there's a doctor handy—for you, not your victim."[42]

> "Feel free to participate in the vampire craze and goth subcultures, but if you're thinking of sampling human blood, make sure there's a doctor handy—for you, not your victim."[42]
>
> —Science-based paranormal investigator Benjamin Radford.

Attraction to the Vampire Lifestyle

People who are not drawn to the vampire lifestyle might wonder what the attraction of this lifestyle is. Psychologists have developed theories that attempt to answer this question. Part of the attraction might be a sense of rejecting society and embracing the darker side of humanity. In other words, some people use vampirism as a way to act on antisocial desires.

Among the first to suggest an association between vampires and antisocial desires was Carl Jung, the founder of analytical

A young woman from France shows off her fangs. She is active in a group whose members share a common interest in vampires and the vampire lifestyle.

psychology. Jung felt that the vampire represented what he called "the shadow," an aspect of the self that the conscious mind suppresses. The shadow contains antisocial impulses as well as immoral motivations and other thoughts, wishes, and fantasies that the conscious mind would consider embarrassing, shameful, or otherwise inappropriate.

Jung's equally prominent rival, father of psychoanalysis Sigmund Freud, felt that a fascination with vampires was instead related to repressed sexuality and aggression and an interest in death and immortality. Freud viewed the vampire as being a means for a person to express deep fears and desires related to sexuality and anger. In other words, he zeroed in on the seductive and brutal nature of vampires. This is understandable, since in the days of Freud and Jung, the vampire was considered so evil that few if any people would consciously choose to live as one.

Freud also felt that subconscious responses to the vampire were associated with the Oedipal complex, which occurs when a child feels rivalry with the parent of the same sex because of a desire for sexual involvement with the parent of the opposite sex. In other words, a boy who feels attracted to his mother and hates his father can be said to have an Oedipal complex. In the 1930s psychoanalyst and neurologist Ernest Jones built on Freud's idea. He suggested that guilt over Oedipal feelings—and the repression of this guilt—could cause both fear of and attraction to vampires, creatures that represent seduction and violence.

Vampire Therapy

In 2014 scientists at Harvard University found that transfusions of young blood can reverse aging and improve brain function. In this study, eighteen-month-old mice—considered elderly based on the fact that a mouse's average life span is two years—were given eight infusions of blood taken from three-month-old mice. Both before and after the infusions, which were given over a period of three weeks, the elderly mice were subjected to tests designed to measure their memories and ability to learn. All showed marked improvement, and researchers subsequently determined that their brains had changed in structural, molecular, and functional ways. In fact, the infusions essentially made the brains younger. Researchers surmise that this transformation is due to the fact that young blood contains much larger amounts of a particular protein than old blood.

The press dubbed this process "vampire therapy." Believers in vampires cite this study as proof that infusions of blood can transform the human body and mind. They liken this to the transformation that supposedly takes place in a human who receives vampire blood and is thus transformed into an immortal vampire.

Doubt

But others say that people are drawn to vampires simply because they are fascinating creatures. In other words, there does not have to be anything wrong with a person—no mental illness, no repressed desires, no physical disease—for that person to be drawn to vampires. This is especially the case, some say, at a time when so many people think of vampires as sensitive, seductive beings rather than as evil monsters. Valerie H, who identifies herself as having a strong interest in vampires, says, "The thought of these bloodsuckers creeping along dark alleys for their next victims not only makes the hair on the back of my neck stand up, but also I find it rather capricious and even rather sexy at times."[43]

> "The thought of these bloodsuckers creeping along dark alleys for their next victims not only makes the hair on the back of my neck stand up, but also I find it rather capricious and even rather sexy at times."[43]
>
> —HubPages author Valerie H.

Valerie H also reports that she once thought she saw a vampire in a bookstore. Dressed in black, he could have been a human, but his skin seemed translucent, his mouth was unnaturally red, and his eyes were piercing. She says, "I don't know if he was a vampire but I did walk away feeling like I had witnessed something not of this world, it was rather creepy but piqued my interest."[44] This kind of doubt—was that or was that not a vampire?—occurs often enough to cause even rational individuals to wonder whether vampires could actually exist.

Source Notes

Introduction: A Distorted Nature

1. Quoted in Jason Colavito, "Vampires, Voltaire 1764," JasonColavito.com. www.jasoncolavito.com.

2. Bram Stoker, *Dracula*, Page by Page Books. www.page bypagebooks.com.

3. Thomas Preskett Prest, *Varney the Vampire; or, the Feast of Blood*, Project Gutenberg. www.gutenberg.org.

4. Mark Collins Jenkins, *Vampire Forensics: Uncovering the Origins of an Enduring Legend*. Washington, DC: National Geographic, 2010, p. 10.

Chapter One: What Attributes Do Vampires Have?

5. Aubrey Sherman, *Vampires: The Myths, Legends, & Lore*. Avon, MA: Adams Media, 2014, p. 12.

6. Quoted in Jenkins, *Vampire Forensics*, p. 115.

7. Quoted in Jenkins, *Vampire Forensics*, pp. 160–61.

8. Konstantinos, *Vampires: The Occult Truth*. Woodbury, MN: Llewellyn, 2010, p. 7.

9. Katherine Ramsland, *The Science of Vampires*. New York: Berkley Boulevard, 2002, p. 89.

10. Alex B. Berezow, "How the Polish Buried Their Vampires," RealClearScience, November 26, 2014. www .realclearscience.com.

11. Quoted in Matthew Beresford, *From Demons to Dracula: The Creation of the Modern Vampire Myth*. London: Reaktion, p. 204.

12. Quoted in Beresford, *From Demons to Dracula*, p. 107.

Chapter Two: Why Do People Believe in Vampires?

13. Quoted in Robert L. Johnson, "The Vampire Archetype," Tallahassee Center for Jungian Studies. http://jungian.info.

14. Quoted in Montague Summers, *Montague Summers' Guide to Vampires*, abridged by Nigel Suckling. www.unicorngarden.com.

15. Quoted in Traci Watson, "'Vampire' Graves Shed Light on Fear of the Undead," *USA Today*, November 29, 2014. www.usatoday.com.

16. Michael E. Bell, "American Vampires and the Ongoing Ambiguity of Death," Intertheory, March 2013. http://intertheory.org.

17. Quoted in Bell, "American Vampires and the Ongoing Ambiguity of Death."

18. Quoted in Bell, "American Vampires and the Ongoing Ambiguity of Death."

19. Quoted in Jenkins, *Vampire Forensics*, p. 137.

20. Quoted in Thomas J. Garza, *The Vampire in Slavic Cultures*. San Diego, CA: Cognella, 2010, p. 20.

21. Quoted in Garza, *The Vampire in Slavic Cultures*, p. 20.

22. Koen Vermeir, "Vampires as 'Creatures of the Imagination' in the Early Modern Period," Academia.edu, 2015. www.academia.edu.

23. Vermeir, "Vampires as 'Creatures of the Imagination' in the Early Modern Period."

24. Quoted in Konstantinos, *Vampires*, p. 90.

25. Quoted in Konstantinos, *Vampires*, p. 91.

Chapter Three: Encounters with Vampires

26. Paul Barber, "Staking Claims: The Vampires of Folklore and Fiction," *Skeptical Enquirer*, March/April 1996. www.csicop .org.

27. Konstantinos, *Vampires*, p. 45.

28. Quoted in Vampirologist, "Encounters with the Highgate Vampire," Vampire Research Society, February 20, 2009. http:// vampireresearchsociety.blogspot.com.

29. Quoted in Vampirologist, "Encounters with the Highgate Vampire."

30. Quoted in Rod McPhee, "Vampire Britain: UK Could Be Home to More Blood-Sucking Nightfeeders than Dracula's Homeland," *Daily Mirror* (London), September 16, 2014. www.mir ror.co.uk.

31. Quoted in Samantha Booth, "Encounter with a Borders Vampire Brought Me into Contact with Michael Jackson, Claims Ghosthunter Tom Robertson," *Daily Record* (Glasgow), September 30, 2012. www.dailyrecord.co.uk.

32. Lynn Gibson, "Jack the Ripper, Case Solved!," *Author Lynn Gibson* (blog), July 24, 2013. https://authorlyngibson.word press.com.

33. Matthew Zarzeczny, "Top Ten Real People Alleged to Be Vampires," TopTenz, August 18, 2013. www.toptenz.net.

34. Zarzeczny, "Top Ten Real People Alleged to Be Vampires."

Chapter Four: Can Science Explain the Belief in Vampires?

35. Quoted in News Staff, "Are Vampires Real? Physics Professor Drives Scientific Stake into the Heart of Supernatural Myths," Science 2.0, October 17, 2007. www.science20.com.

36. Ramsland, *The Science of Vampires*, pp. 22–23.

37. Ramsland, *The Science of Vampires*, p. 29.

38. Jenkins, *Vampire Forensics*, p. 17.

39. Ramsland, *The Science of Vampires*, p. 97.

40. Quoted in *Daily Mail* (London), "Teenager Guilty of Pensioner's 'Vampire Ritual' Killing," March 5, 2015. www.dailymail.co.uk.

41. Quoted in Ramsland, *The Science of Vampires*, p. 31.

42. Benjamin Radford, "Is It Safe to Drink Blood?," LiveScience, September 2, 2011. www.livescience.com.

43. Valerie H, "Why Are Vampires So Interesting?," HubPages, March 20, 2011. http://valerieh.hubpages.com.

44. Valerie H, "Why Are Vampires So Interesting?"

For Further Research

Books

Matthew Bunson, *The Vampire Encyclopedia*. New York: Gramercy, 2000.

Charles River Editors, *The History and Folklore of Vampires: The Stories and Legends Behind the Mythical Beings*. Seattle: CreateSpace, 2014. Kindle edition.

Radu Florescu and Raymond T. McNally, *In Search of Dracula: The History of Dracula and Vampires*. New York: Houghton Mifflin, 1994.

Claude Leconteaux, *The Secret History of Vampires: Their Multiple Forms and Hidden Purposes*. Rochester, VT: Inner Traditions, 2010.

J. Gordon Melton, *The Vampire Book: The Encyclopedia of the Undead*, 3rd ed. Canton, MI: Visible Ink, 2011.

Aubrey Sherman, *Vampires: The Myths, Legends, & Lore*. Avon, MA: Adams Media, 2014.

Montague Summers, *Vampires and Vampirism*. Mineola, NY: Dover, 2005. First published 1929 by Dutton.

Internet Sources

Tori E. Godfree, "Vampires: The Ever-Changing Face of Fear," *Student Pulse*, 2010. www.studentpulse.com/articles/247 /vampires-the-ever-changing-face-of-fear.

Random Facts, "40 Interesting Facts About Vampires," May 2, 2009. http://facts.randomhistory.com/2009/05/02_vampires.html.

Abigail Tucker, "The Great New England Vampire Panic," *Smithsonian*, October 2012. www.smithsonianmag.com/history/the-great-new-england-vampire-panic-36482878/?no-ist=&page=3.

Abigail Tucker, "Meet the Real-Life Vampires of New England and Abroad," *Smithsonian*, October 2012. www.smithsonianmag.com/history/meet-the-real-life-vampires-of-new-england-and-abroad-42639093/?no-ist.

Index

Picture Credits

About the Author

Patricia D. Netzley is the author of dozens of books for children, teens, and adults. She writes both fiction and nonfiction and is a member of the Society of Children's Book Writers and Illustrators.